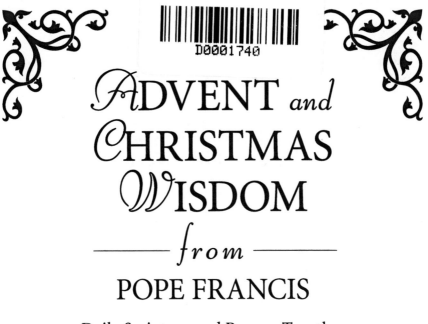

$\mathcal{A}$DVENT *and* $\mathcal{C}$HRISTMAS $\mathcal{W}$ISDOM

—— *from* ——

POPE FRANCIS

Daily Scripture and Prayers Together
With Pope Francis' Own Words

John Cleary

Liguori

Imprimi Potest:
Stephen T. Rehrauer, CSsR, Provincial, Denver Province, the Redemptorists

Published by Liguori Publications, Liguori, Missouri 63057
To order, visit Liguori.org or call 800-325-9521.

Library of Congress Cataloging-in-Publication Data

Cleary, John J.
Advent and Christmas wisdom from Pope Francis / John Cleary.
    pages cm
  ISBN 978-0-7648-2646-7
  1. Advent—Prayers and devotions. 2. Christmas—Prayers and devotions.
  3. Catholic Church—Prayers and devotions. 4. Francis, Pope, 1936–Quotations.
  I. Title.
  BX2170.A4C64 2015
  242'.33—dc23
                            2015020533
  p ISBN: 978-0-7648-2646-7 / e ISBN: 978-0-7648-7078-1

Liguori Publications, a nonprofit corporation, is an apostolate of the Redemptorists. To learn more about the Redemptorists, visit Redemptorists.com.

Printed in the United States of America
19 18 17 16 15 / 5 4 3 2 1
First Edition

Contents

To my son and daughter,
Joseph and Elizabeth Cleary

A Path for Advent and Christmas

Perhaps one of the lesser-known titles by which a pope is known is "Servant of the servants of God," which makes it clear that his role is one of service to us, the Universal Church: every man, woman, and child baptized into the Roman Catholic Church. The pope is—first and foremost—a servant, lowering himself in stature, humbling himself in the manner of Jesus when he arrived among us more than 2,000 years ago in the little village of Bethlehem. Pope Francis seems to embrace this title, does he not? The papacy under Francis seems vacant of any sense of self-importance.

When he named himself after that revered saint—truly a man of the poor who emptied himself of every aspect of ego—our Holy Father embraced the reputation of St. Francis of Assisi by reflecting the lifestyle and outlook of one of the greatest saints in our Church's history. Just as Jesus was born into poverty and called his followers to be "poor in spirit" (reliant on God for every need) so also does Pope Francis stress this deep spirituality. Saint Francis professed it and lived it, as did another great saint of the Church: Thérèse of Lisieux. Is it any surprise that Pope Francis is such a devotee of the Little Flower? In her autobiography, *The Story of a Soul*, St. Thérèse wrote countless times about becoming "small" for the Lord, that is, ever more reliant on all aspects of what he provides.

When *Time* named him 2013 "Person of the Year," the magazine called Francis "the People's Pope." A better moniker could not be assigned. Just as Jesus—born in a manger to a family of marginal means—allied himself with the poor, Pope Francis embraces a poverty that does not allow for any unnecessary baggage or "spiritual worldliness." He embraces a lifestyle reliant completely on the Lord, without the distraction of worldly treasure and the self-centeredness those treasures attract.

Being poor in spirit means relying fully on our Lord and Savior, Jesus Christ, whose arrival we await with great anticipation during this Advent and Christmas season. In the days to come, we have much to learn from our Holy Father about faith and relying wholly on God throughout all of our daily lives.

Asceticism is the way of life our Holy Father embraces: simple apartments and other earmarks of a sparse earthly life. He seeks only those things that strengthen his relationship with God—and it is on God alone upon whom he relies for the basic necessities he requires to serve the Lord with his complete person. Pope Francis asks the same of his fellow priests and all religious throughout the world, as well as lay Catholics. His teaching and example of holiness has been received with great enthusiasm by all sectors of the faithful during his papacy, as well as by people outside the Catholic Church and Christianity.

Throughout this Advent and Christmas journey, we will explore the wellspring of humility and generosity that serve as the hallmarks of our fervent and devout Holy Father. The spirituality of Pope Francis is a unique combination of all the best aspects of the Society of Jesus (self-discipline, asceticism, and austerity) and the deep faithfulness to poverty and total reliance on God of St. Francis of Assisi. May the holy words of our beloved Francis guide us along our own path to greater nearness and devotion to our Savior, and may our loving Jesus draw us closer to him as we anticipate his coming and contemplate the salvific beauty of the great mystery of the Incarnation.

Know also, dear readers, that your spiritual growth and welfare are committed to my own prayers as you proceed along this worthy Advent and Christmas journey.

John Cleary
St. Louis, 2015

A Chronology of the Life of Pope Francis

December 17, 1936 •	Jorge Mario Bergoglio is born in Buenos Aires, Argentina, to Mario José Bergoglio, an Italian immigrant, and Regina Maria Sivori of Argentina.
December 1957 •	At age 21, he falls gravely ill; severe pneumonia is diagnosed and part of his right lung is removed. He recovers fully and decides to devote himself to the priesthood.
March 11, 1958 •	Enters the novitiate of the Society of Jesus
March 12, 1960 •	Takes his first vows as a Jesuit
1961–1963 •	Studies philosophy at San Miguel Seminary in Buenos Aires
1967–1970 •	Studies theology at San Miguel Seminary
December 13, 1969 •	Ordained priest
1973 •	Takes perpetual profession as Jesuit
1973–1979 •	Serves as superior of Jesuit province of Argentina and Uruguay
June 27, 1992 •	Fr. Jorge, as he is known, is ordained Auxiliary Bishop of Buenos Aires.
February 28, 1998 •	Installed as Archbishop of Buenos Aires
2001 •	Co-presides over Synod of Bishops
February 21, 2001 •	Elevated to cardinal
2005–2011 •	Serves as president, Argentine Bishops Conference
March 13, 2013 •	Elected 266th pope of the Catholic Church, he is the first Holy Father from the Americas, the first Jesuit, and the first to take the name Francis.
September 2015 •	He makes first papal visit to the United States, attending the 2015 World Meeting of Families in Philadelphia.

How to Use This Book

*A*dvent—that period of great anticipatory joy—is a time of preparation for the celebration of Jesus' arrival in Bethlehem as a helpless infant. In Western liturgy, Advent begins four Sundays before December 25—the Sunday closest to November 30, which is the feast of St. Andrew, Jesus' first disciple.

The annual commemoration of Jesus' birth begins the Christmas cycle of the liturgical year—a cycle that runs from Christmas Eve to the Sunday after the feast of the Epiphany. In keeping with the unfolding of the message of the liturgical year, this book is designed to be used during the entire period from the first Sunday of Advent to the end of the Christmas cycle.

The four weeks of Advent are often thought of as symbolizing the four different ways that Jesus comes into the world: (1) his birth as a helpless infant at Bethlehem, (2) his arrival in the hearts of believers, (3) his death, and (4) his coming on Judgment Day.

Because Christmas falls on a different day of the week each year, the fourth week of Advent is never finished; it is abruptly, joyously, and solemnly abrogated by the annual celebration of the coming of Jesus at Christmas. Likewise, Christ's Second Coming will abruptly interrupt our sojourn on earth.

Since the calendar dictates the number of days in Advent, this book includes Scripture and meditation readings for a full twenty-eight days. These twenty-eight daily readings make up Part I of this book. It is suggested that the reader begin at the beginning and, on Christmas, switch to Part II, which contains materials for the twelve days of Christmas. I suggest that any extra entries from Part I may be read by doubling up days or by reading two entries on weekends. Alternately, one may just skip these entries that do not fit within the Advent time frame for that particular year.

Each daily entry in this book begins with the words of Pope Francis taken from encyclicals, letters, homilies, speeches, and interviews. His addresses were given in Vatican City, unless noted otherwise. Following each quotation is an excerpt from Scripture, which is related in some way to the pope's quote. Next is a small prayer, also built on the ideas from the two preceding passages. Finally, I suggest an Advent or Christmas activity as a way to apply the messages to your daily life.

PART I

~

READINGS *for* ADVENT

$\mathcal{D}$ay

1

We Are a Gift to One Another

$\mathcal{W}$e cannot live without facing challenges, without responding to challenges. Whoever does not face challenges, whoever does not take up challenges, is not living. Your willingness and your abilities, combined with the power of the Holy Spirit who abides in each of us from the day of baptism, allow you to be more than mere spectators, they allow you to be protagonists in contemporary events. Please do not watch life go by from the balcony! Mingle where the challenges are calling you to help carry life and development forward, in the struggle over human dignity, in the fight against poverty, in the battle for values and in the many battles we encounter each day....May the commitment to journeying in faith and behaving in a manner consistent with the Gospel accompany you this Advent Season.

Francis' Homily, Celebration of Vespers with Students of Roman Athenums, Vatican Basilica, First Sunday of Advent, November 30, 2013

Scripture

The end of all things is at hand. Therefore, be serious and sober for prayers. Above all, let your love for one another be intense, because love covers a multitude of sins. Be hospitable to one another without complaining. As each one has received a gift, use it to serve one another as good stewards of God's varied grace. Whoever preaches, let it be with the words of God; whoever serves, let it be with the strength that God supplies, so that in all things God may be glorified through Jesus Christ, to whom belong glory and dominion forever and ever. Amen.

1 Peter 4:7–11

Prayer

Good and generous God, you give me everything I have and everything I need. You have loved me into existence as part of your divine plan, you have blessed me with unique gifts, and you have graced me with patience and perseverance as I have honed and developed these gifts so as to praise your name, comfort others, and glorify your creation on earth. May I be a gift from you to everyone I meet. I pray that the challenges I encounter deepen my bond with you as I employ those gifts and talents with which you have graced me in overcoming these challenges. May my efforts require your grace all the more and, in doing so, bring me ever closer to you in the relationship we share. Amen.

ADVENT ACTION

So often we hear (or say to ourselves) that the Christmas season has become so commercialized through the buying and giving of presents that its true meaning has been lost. That point is well made, as commercials tell us to hustle to the mall and buy jewelry for her, a bike for him, or the latest-and-greatest techno gadget for them. However, let us remember that Christmas is indeed about gift giving. What gift was given to us beneath a star in a manger more than 2,000 years ago? Forget about the material gifts and remember the *real* gift: God giving himself to us through the Incarnation.

For the next five to ten minutes, reflect on yourself as a gift to those in your life. In how many ways and to how many people can you—throughout this Advent and Christmas season—become a gift from God to those you know and to those you do not?

Day

2

Create an Open Space Within

*T*he great danger in today's world, pervaded as it is by consumerism, is the desolation and anguish born of a complacent yet covetous heart, the feverish pursuit of frivolous pleasures, and a blunted conscience. Whenever our interior life becomes caught up in its own interests and concerns, there is no longer room for others, no place for the poor....

I invite all Christians, everywhere, at this very moment, to a renewed personal encounter with Jesus Christ, or at least an openness to letting him encounter them; I ask all of you to do this unfailingly each day. No one should think that this invitation is not meant for him or her, since "no one is excluded from the joy brought by the Lord" (Paul VI, Apostolic Exhortation *Gaudete in Domino*, May 9, 1975). The Lord does not disappoint those who take this risk; whenever we take a step toward Jesus, we come to realize that he is already there, waiting for us with open arms.

FRANCIS' APOSTOLIC EXHORTATION *EVANGELII GAUDIUM*, 2–3,
NOVEMBER 24, 2013

SCRIPTURE

A clean heart create for me, God;
renew within me a steadfast spirit.
Do not drive me from before your face,
nor take from me your holy spirit...
For you do not desire sacrifice or I would give it;
a burnt offering you would not accept.
My sacrifice, O God, is a contrite spirit;
a contrite, humbled heart, O God, you will not scorn.

PSALM 51:12–13; 18–19

PRAYER

God of action and passionate love, your grace surrounds us, awaiting the smallest crevice by which to enter and break down the walls that divide us. Our free will is a great gift from you. It allows us to freely choose the good—the greatest good—over everything that is less. Let us seek our pleasure in the Lord, the greatest of all goods, and not in lesser things that wither and die. You desire action from me, love in action; not words and empty promises. Lord, may my life be one of action, where everything I have to give I give with a commitment to you, with an aim toward the ever-deepening communion you seek between you and your creation. Amen.

Advent Action

A quote often attributed to St. Francis of Assisi is this beauty: "Preach the Gospel at all times. Use words if necessary." Whether he actually said this or not is open to question, but what a challenge to those of us who enjoy dispensing advice, talking incessantly about what we could do or should do, and judging the words and actions of others. How much harder is it to evangelize without words or open our hearts to God's grace and allow that power to energize and activate our love for God?

Today or tomorrow, open your heart and let God's grace guide your actions and feed your courage when you see an opportunity to act as Jesus would toward a person in need. The grace of God's love will guide you when the time is right; you need only be open to it.

$\mathcal{D}$ay

3

The Light of Faith Is Our Star

$\mathcal{T}$he light of Faith: this is how the Church's tradition speaks of the great gift brought by Jesus. In John's Gospel, Christ says of himself: "I have come as light into the world, that whoever believes in me may not remain in darkness" (John 12:46). Saint Paul uses the same image: "God who said 'Let light shine out of darkness,' has shone in our hearts" (2 Corinthians 4:6). The pagan world, which hungered for light, had seen the growth of the cult of the sun god, *Sol Invictus,* invoked each day at sunrise. Yet though the sun was born anew each morning, it was clearly incapable of casting its light on all of human existence. The sun does not illumine all reality; its rays cannot penetrate to the shadow of death, the place where men's eyes are closed to its light. "No one—Saint Justin Martyr writes— has ever been ready to die for his faith in the sun" (*Dialogus cum Tryphone Iudaeo,* 121, 2: PG 6, 758)....Those who believe, see; they see with a light that illumines their entire journey, for it comes from the risen Christ, the morning star which never sets.

FRANCIS' ENCYCLICAL LETTER *LUMEN FIDEI*, 1,
JUNE 29, 2013

Scripture

After their audience with the king they set out. And behold, the star that they had seen at its rising preceded them, until it came and stopped over the place where the child was. They were overjoyed at seeing the star, and on entering the house they saw the child with Mary his mother. They prostrated themselves and did him homage. Then they opened their treasures and offered him gifts of gold, frankincense, and myrrh.

MATTHEW 2:9–11

Prayer

Innocent and holy Infant Jesus, as we await the celebration of your birth, we see there are many lights in the night sky that attract our attention, sometimes enticing us away from you. When we see a dazzling array of gifts, our selfish nature shifts our attention back onto ourselves and away from you. During this holy season of Advent we ask that you keep our eyes trained on the star that leads to you, where we might contemplate the holy mystery of the Incarnation, that moment in history when God reunited with man and overcame the rift of sin that had divided us for so long. May we find Jesus where we seek him and may we do him homage when we find him. May we always follow the true light of Christ and never the lesser or artificial lights that lead us astray. Amen.

ADVENT ACTION

This Advent season, pay particular attention to those "false lights" that often insidiously distract us from the True Light, the coming of the Christ Child. Stay alert! Beware! It's more than just television commercials, the demands of our electronic devices, and window shopping. Sometimes it's gossip masquerading as idle parish conversation. There are myriad bells and whistles, enticements and desires that draw our attention away from what should be the priority of this liturgical season—the deepening of our relationship with Jesus.

Before you react to an enticement, ask yourself if this is something that brings you closer to God and deepens your intimacy with him as your friend.

Day

4

Jesus Is With Us in Our Suffering and Sorrow

The presence of God among men did not take place in a perfect, idyllic world but rather in this real world, which is marked by so many things both good and bad, by division, wickedness, poverty, arrogance and war. He chose to live in our history as it is, with all the weight of its limitations and of its tragedies. In doing so, he has demonstrated in an unequalled manner his merciful and truly loving disposition toward the human creature. He is God-with-us. Jesus is God-with-us. Do you believe this? Together let us profess: Jesus is God with us! Jesus is God with us always and forever with us in history's suffering and sorrow. The Birth of Jesus reveals that God "sided" with man once and for all, to save us, to raise us from the dust of our misery, from our difficulty, from our sins.

FRANCIS, GENERAL AUDIENCE, ST. PETER'S SQUARE,
DECEMBER 18, 2013

Scripture

And the Word became flesh
and made his dwelling among us,
and we saw his glory,
the glory as of the Father's only Son,
full of grace and truth.

JOHN 1:14

Prayer

Holy Father, you sent your only Son for our salvation—that's how much you love us. That's how much you desired to make whole what was broken by man's original sin. Jesus arrived in this world as a person of very little means, into a humble family living among the poor, the uneducated, and the lost. We were sent a shepherd for lost sheep, a doctor for those in need of healing. He revealed your glory and your love for mankind throughout his life and by his death. By his resurrection, death and sin were defeated. Every aspect of human existence was made sacred, including death, and the Father's desire to share life with his creation after death was completed through the Son. For this love we proclaim the name and the love of God in word and deed. Amen.

Sometime today or tomorrow, find ten minutes of quiet time and reread John 1:6–18. Even though he only appears in the New Testament, John the Baptist is often referred to as the last prophet of the Old Testament. He is the final prophet to precede Jesus and he testifies to Jesus' glory. Reflect during this time on the deep, deep love our Creator has for you that he would share in our human condition through the Incarnation and dwell with us in his earthly life to reveal the love and desire of his Father in heaven, that—if only we have faith and believe in the Son—we will sit in the Father's presence for all eternity. Reflect on the desire for relationship God has for you, the love he has for you, and the want for intimate friendship in this life and in the next.

𝒟ay

5

Growth in Communion Through Sacraments, Charisms, and Charity

We grow in unity, in communion, through the Sacraments, the charisms given to each of us by the Holy Spirit, and charity.

First of all, the communion of the Sacraments. The Sacraments express and realize an effective and profound communion among us, for in them we encounter Christ the Saviour and, through him, our brothers and sisters in faith....A second aspect of communion in holy things is the communion of charisms. The Holy Spirit distributes to the faithful a multitude of spiritual gifts and graces.... The charisms...are gifts that the Holy Spirit gives us, talents, possibilities....Gifts given not to be hidden but to be shared with others. [Then] we come to the third aspect of communion in holy things, that is, communion in charity, the unity among us that creates charity, love.

FRANCIS, GENERAL AUDIENCE, ST. PETER'S SQUARE,
NOVEMBER 6, 2013

SCRIPTURE

Love never fails. If there are prophecies, they will be brought to nothing; if tongues, they will cease; if knowledge, it will be brought to nothing. For we know partially and we prophesy partially, but when the perfect comes, the partial will pass away. When I was a child, I used to talk as a child, think as a child, reason as a child; when I became a man, I put aside childish things. At present we see indistinctly, as in a mirror, but then face to face. At present I know partially; then I shall know fully, as I am fully known. So faith, hope, love remain, these three; but the greatest of these is love.

1 CORINTHIANS 13:8–13

PRAYER

Lord God, we often speak of growing in communion, in intimate friendship, with you. Sometimes we view the world as too filthy a place for such unity. We might even believe such closeness with you can be fostered only within a vacuum, separate from this world with all of its shortcomings. Then we recall that you, as divine, entered this world, nurtured friendships, and revealed love daily among every sort of person. You showed us the way. Our communion with you is deepened through the pleasure of our communion with our brothers and sisters. Whether it is through the sacraments, charisms, or charity, when we deepen our communion with other believers we deepen our communion with you, the one in whose image we are all made. You show us how we are to love others, and you grace us with the ability to do so. Amen.

ADVENT ACTION

Fostering communion with our fellow brothers and sisters is at times gratifying, challenging, spiritually deepening, frustrating, fun, or just plain hard work.

Reflect on the ways in which you foster communion with your parish community. Are there any gifts of the Holy Spirit you're holding back for any reason? Perhaps you're not even aware you have certain gifts. Spend time in prayer today or tomorrow, considering all the gifts you've been given. Perhaps you focus more on some than others. Consider the simplest gifts you can offer another: your presence, your ability to listen, your support and encouragement, your smile, your prayer, your attention, or your caring.

Day

6

The Danger of Worldliness

$\mathcal{T}$oday [the Church] must strip herself of a very grave danger, which threatens every person in the Church, everyone: the danger of worldliness. The Christian cannot coexist with the spirit of the world, with the worldliness that leads us to vanity, to arrogance, to pride. And this is an idol, it is not God. It is an idol! And idolatry is the gravest of sins!

Many of you have been stripped by this callous world that offers no work, no help. To this world it doesn't matter that there are children dying of hunger; it doesn't matter if many families have nothing to eat, do not have the dignity of bringing bread home; it doesn't matter that many people are forced to flee slavery, hunger and flee in search of freedom. With how much pain, how often don't we see that they meet death[.] The spirit of the world causes these things. It is unthinkable that a Christian—a true Christian—be it a priest, a sister, a bishop, a cardinal or a Pope, would want to go down this path of worldliness!

FRANCIS' PASTORAL VISIT TO ASSISI, MEETING WITH POOR ASSISTED BY CARITAS, ROOM OF RENUNCIATION OF THE ARCHBISHOP'S RESIDENCE, ASSISI, OCTOBER 4, 2013

Scripture

*"Do not store up for yourselves treasures on earth, where moth
and decay destroy, and thieves break in and steal. But store up
treasures in heaven, where neither moth nor decay destroys,
nor thieves break in and steal. For where your treasure is, there
also will your heart be."*

MATTHEW 6:19–21

Prayer

Good and loving God, you know that sometimes I worry. I
worry about myself—am I good enough? I worry about my
family—what do they need that I can help to give? I worry
about having enough—do I have enough stored up on this
earth to ensure the security of my family? How much of
what I need and what my family needs do I entrust to you?
Am I always making myself the center, calling myself to task
to carry the load? Worldliness is a dangerous trap, easy to
slide into if I am not careful. Make me more aware of your
priority in my life. May I always be at the service of the one
master that is you, my Lord and my God, even as I dwell in
the practical aspects of family needs and home economics.
This grace of wisdom I ask of you, dear Lord. Amen.

ADVENT ACTION

Today take ten to fifteen minutes of quiet time to take stock of your working life—at school, at work, at home with finance and the needs of your family. How invested is your faith in these "practical" aspects of your day-to-day life? Do you think of God and seek his guidance and peace while you balance your checkbook?

Keep aware of your priorities, especially in the midst of the mundane or seemingly secular facets of your life. This is how worldliness can creep in. You mistakenly remove God from areas of your life that seem to have no place for him. Your life is a prayer, and every part of it calls out to make God a priority.

Day

7

The Light of Our Lord Is the Truth

*I*n speaking of the light of faith, we can almost hear the objections of many of our contemporaries....[T]hat light might have been considered sufficient for societies of old, but was felt to be of no use for new times, for a humanity come of age, proud of its rationality and anxious to explore the future in novel ways.... Slowly but surely, however, it would become evident that the light of autonomous reason is not enough to illumine the future; ultimately the future remains shadowy and fraught with fear of the unknown. As a result, humanity renounced the search for a great light, Truth itself, in order to be content with smaller lights which illumine the fleeting moment yet prove incapable of showing the way. Yet in the absence of light everything becomes confused; it is impossible to tell good from evil, or the road to our destination from other roads which take us in endless circles, going nowhere.

FRANCIS' ENCYCLICAL LETTER *LUMEN FIDEI*, 3,
JUNE 29, 2013

SCRIPTURE

"How can you say, 'Show us the Father'? Do you not believe that I am in the Father and the Father is in me? The words that I speak to you I do not speak on my own. The Father who dwells in me is doing his works. Believe me that I am in the Father and the Father is in me, or else, believe because of the works themselves. Amen, amen, I say to you, whoever believes in me will do the works that I do, and will do greater ones than these, because I am going to the Father. And whatever you ask in my name, I will do, so that the Father may be glorified in the Son. If you ask anything of me in my name, I will do it."

JOHN 14:9–14

PRAYER

God of light, who illuminates our reason and deepens our wisdom, guide our path to truth and knowledge through your Son, Jesus. Grace us with the courage and wisdom to hold fast to our faith, and allow that faith to guide us in our pursuit of reason. We know you are the source of all truth, that you have revealed that truth through your Son, and that by having faith in your Son we will reach the Father, Son, and Holy Spirit in the afterlife. As believers, we know faith and reason go hand-in-hand, one with the other. Faith and reason cannot contradict one another; there is only one truth. Grace us, Lord and friend, with a perseverance to seek the truth—wisdom and reason—armored in our faith. Where there is darkness may our faith in you and your fidelity to us reveal every truth. Amen.

ADVENT ACTION

Today is a good day to open up your copy of the *Catechism of the Catholic Church (CCC)*. If you don't have a copy, borrow one, buy a copy, or pull it up online. The truths presented in the *Catechism* are irrefutable. This is reason illuminated by faith.

On this day, take ten minutes to read, reflect, and pray on the topic of faith and reason, and the light of faith that illuminates our path in our pursuit of the ultimate truth. For today, read and reflect on *Catechism* paragraph 159. Compare its words to today's message from Pope Francis.

Day

8

God Desires a Personal Relationship With Us

*F*aith opens the way before us and accompanies our steps through time. Hence, if we want to understand what faith is, we need to follow the route it has taken, the path trodden by believers, as witnessed first in the Old Testament. Here a unique place belongs to Abraham, our father in faith. Something disturbing takes place in his life: God speaks to him; he reveals himself as a God who speaks and calls his name. Faith is linked to hearing. Abraham does not see God, but hears his voice. Faith thus takes on a personal aspect. God is not the god of a particular place, or a deity linked to specific sacred time, but the God of a person, the God of Abraham, Isaac and Jacob, capable of interacting with man and establishing a covenant with him. Faith is our response to a word which engages us personally, to a "Thou" who calls us by name.

FRANCIS' ENCYCLICAL LETTER *LUMEN FIDEI*, 8,
JUNE 29, 2013

SCRIPTURE

Abram continued, "Look, you have given me no offspring, so a servant of my household will be my heir." Then the word of the LORD came to him: No, that one will not be your heir; your own offspring will be your heir. He took him outside and said: Look up at the sky and count the stars, if you can. Just so, he added, will your descendants be. Abram put his faith in the LORD, who attributed it to him as an act of righteousness.

GENESIS 15:3–6

PRAYER

Dearest Lord Jesus, you who seeks friendship with us today just as your Father did with his faithful servant Abraham, we welcome this intimate relationship. You have revealed everything to us in trust, just as one dear friend reveals to another. You know me better than I know myself; even when I try to hide my true self from you or from others, you know my heart and reach out to me in a spirit of loving trust and the deepest friendship. You grace me with the courage to be true to who I am—admitting my faults, acknowledging my sins, and embracing my limitations, my humanity, my need for you. Grace me today to take your hand in friendship, to rely on you to direct my path, and to grant me the fortitude to do what you call me to do. Amen.

ADVENT ACTION

In the Gospel of John 15:15, Jesus says the following to his disciples: "I no longer call you slaves, because a slave does not know what his master is doing. I have called you friends, because I have told you everything I have heard from my Father."

Call to my mind some friends of yours. How did your relationship originate? As coworkers? Students? Neighbors? Spend ten to fifteen minutes in prayer. Lift these friends up to God; pray that your friends in heaven bless and grace your friends on earth. For what will you petition God on their behalf? In what ways can you advocate that these friends experience a deeper friendship with the Blessed Trinity?

Day

9

Hope Begins With Obedience

he word spoken to Abraham contains both a call and a promise. First, it is a call to leave his own land, a summons to a new life, the beginning of an exodus which points him toward an unforeseen future. The sight which faith would give to Abraham would always be linked to the need to take this step forward: faith "sees" to the extent that it journeys, to the extent that it chooses to enter into the horizons opened up by God's word. This word also contains a promise: Your descendants will be great in number, you will be the father of a great nation (see Genesis 13:16; 15:5; 22:17). As a response to a word which preceded it, Abraham's faith would always be an act of remembrance. Yet this remembrance is not fixed on past events but, as the memory of a promise, it becomes capable of opening up the future, shedding light on the path to be taken. We see how faith, as remembrance of the future, *memoria futuri*, is thus closely bound up with hope.

FRANCIS' ENCYCLICAL LETTER *LUMEN FIDEI*, 9,
JUNE 29, 2013

Scripture

[Jesus] saw two boats there alongside the lake; the fishermen had disembarked and were washing their nets. Getting into one of the boats, the one belonging to Simon, he asked him to put out a short distance from the shore. Then he sat down and taught the crowds from the boat. After he had finished speaking, he said to Simon, "Put out into deep water and lower your nets for a catch." Simon said in reply, "Master, we have worked hard all night and have caught nothing, but at your command I will lower the nets." When they had done this, they caught a great number of fish and their nets were tearing.

LUKE 5:2–6

Prayer

Loving Jesus, your only desire is for our joy. And we are able to attain this joy through your grace in obedience to your word. For though you call us friends, we are not equals. You are still our Lord and master, and we serve you, yet by your desire and our own we come to know one another in the intimate fashion of friends. May our obedience to your word increase our faith for the future, a future place in heaven you have designed and built especially for us to abide for all time. Amen.

ADVENT ACTION

Today contemplate these Scripture verses from St. Paul's Letter to the Romans: "But thanks be to God that, although you were once slaves of sin, you have become obedient from the heart to the pattern of teaching to which you were entrusted. Freed from sin, you have become slaves of righteousness." How is it that a slave can be free? Freed from sin, you are a slave to (that is, bound to, embraced by) righteousness. You are a servant to the Lord. You love him so much you cannot help but choose to follow.

What specific anxiety about your future are you rolling over and over in your thoughts these days? Speak it out loud to God. Do not be a slave to fear. Share this intimate friendship with God, embrace his grace, and allow him to take on your burden. Enjoy the freedom that accompanies slavery to righteousness.

Day

10

Putting Jesus in the First Place

*F*rancis [of Assisi] divested himself of everything, before his father, before the Bishop, and the people of Assisi. It was a prophetic gesture, and it was also an act of prayer, an act of love and of trust to the Father who is in Heaven. With this gesture Francis made his choice: the choice to be poor. That is not a sociological, ideological choice, it is a choice to be like Jesus, to imitate him, to follow him to the end....

The renunciation of St. Francis tells us simply what the Gospel teaches: following Jesus means putting him in first place, stripping ourselves of the many things that we possess that suffocate our hearts, renouncing ourselves, taking up the cross and carrying it with Jesus.

FRANCIS' PASTORAL VISIT TO ASSISI, MEETING WITH POOR ASSISTED BY
CARITAS, ROOM OF RENUNCIATION OF THE ARCHBISHOP'S RESIDENCE,
ASSISI, OCTOBER 4, 2013

SCRIPTURE

The young man said to him, "All of these I have observed. What do I still lack?" Jesus said to him, "If you wish to be perfect, go, sell what you have and give to [the] poor, and you will have treasure in heaven. Then come, follow me." When the young man heard this statement, he went away sad, for he had many possessions.

MATTHEW 19:20–22

PRAYER

Lord God, my Savior and my Redeemer, your will is what I seek; my will offers no satisfaction. Just as St. Francis stripped himself of everything—his money, his clothing, his social status—as a gesture of giving himself over completely to your will, move me to do the same in my own way. During this Advent and Christmas season, may I divest myself of those attachments that seek only to serve my will at the expense of your will and at the expense of my earthly and eternal happiness. Your ways are not my own, and though I may not understand the consequence or end of what you are asking me to do, may I be graced with the courage to act according to your word so I may seek you and only you. Amen.

ADVENT ACTION

Let's consider first part of the traditional Serenity Prayer:

God, grant me the serenity
to accept the things I cannot change,
the courage to change the things I can,
and wisdom to know the difference.

REINHOLD NIEBUHR (1892–1971)

With pen and paper, list those things in your life you cannot change (and must accept) and then list those matters/issues you would like to change, aided by the grace of fortitude. See what parts of your life you can strip away (in the manner of St. Francis) that will align you with God's will rather than your own and then make it a point to act on that knowledge by seeking the same grace of courage by which God empowered St. Francis.

Day 11

We Should Continually Encounter Jesus

lways remember this: life is a journey. It is a path, a journey to meet Jesus. At the end, and forever. A journey in which we do not encounter Jesus is not a Christian journey. It is for the Christian to continually encounter Jesus, to watch him, to let himself be watched over by Jesus, because Jesus watches us with love; he loves us so much, he loves us so much and he is always watching over us. To encounter Jesus also means allowing oneself to be gazed upon by him. "But, Father," one of you might say to me, "you know that this journey is horrible for me, I am such a sinner, I have committed many sins...how can I encounter Jesus?" And you know that the people whom Jesus most sought out were the greatest sinners....And along the way Jesus comes and forgives us.

FRANCIS' HOMILY DURING PASTORAL VISIT TO THE ROMAN PARISH
OF ST. CYRIL OF ALEXANDRIA, FIRST SUNDAY OF ADVENT,
DECEMBER 1, 2013

SCRIPTURE

When the disciples saw him walking on the sea they were terrified. "It is a ghost," they said, and they cried out in fear. At once [Jesus] spoke to them, "Take courage, it is I; do not be afraid." Peter said to him in reply, "Lord, if it is you, command me to come to you on the water." He said, "Come." Peter got out of the boat and began to walk on the water toward Jesus. But when he saw how [strong] the wind was he became frightened; and, beginning to sink, he cried out, "Lord, save me!" Immediately Jesus stretched out his hand and caught him, and said to him, "O you of little faith, why did you doubt?" After they got into the boat, the wind died down. Those who were in the boat did him homage, saying, "Truly, you are the Son of God."

MATTHEW 14:26–33

PRAYER

Jesus, my healer and friend, you are with me at all times on my life's journey. Be it smooth roads or rocky ground, you walk beside me—and carry me—along my way. You watch my every step, you gaze lovingly upon me as I rest, and you help me to my feet when I fall. May the Holy Spirit strengthen my resolve and grace me with courage to encounter you, my friend Jesus, without compromise and with full intimacy. May I offer everything I am to you alone. Although I will falter at times, sinking into the depths when I take my eyes off you, you will reach out your hand, I will take hold of it, and our journey will continue until the end, and forever. Amen.

ADVENT ACTION

As a spiritual exercise for the day, focus your attention on the fact that Jesus is right beside you, gazing lovingly at you and encouraging you as you go about your day. Be mindful about how this reality affects your behavior throughout your day. How does having your best friend, your healer, your Savior, and your biggest supporter by your side alter the way you encounter others, be it family, friends, strangers, or those people you struggle to love?

Day

12

Tis the Season to Celebrate New Life

A final element of the story of Abraham is important for understanding his faith. God's word, while bringing newness and surprise, is not at all alien to Abraham's experience. In the voice which speaks to him, the patriarch recognizes a profound call which was always present at the core of his being. God ties his promise to that aspect of human life which has always appeared most "full of promise," namely, parenthood, the begetting of new life: "Sarah your wife shall bear you a son, and you shall name him Isaac" (Genesis 17:19). The God who asks Abraham for complete trust reveals himself to be the source of all life. Faith is thus linked to God's fatherhood, which gives rise to all creation; the God who calls Abraham is the Creator, the one who "calls into existence the things that do not exist" (Romans 4:17).

FRANCIS' ENCYCLICAL LETTER LUMEN FIDEI, 11,
JUNE 29, 2013

SCRIPTURE

In the sixth month, the angel Gabriel was sent from God to a town of Galilee called Nazareth, to a virgin betrothed to a man named Joseph, of the house of David, and the virgin's name was Mary. And coming to her, he said, "Hail, favored one! The Lord is with you." But she was greatly troubled at what was said and pondered what sort of greeting this might be. Then the angel said to her, "Do not be afraid, Mary, for you have found favor with God. Behold, you will conceive in your womb and bear a son, and you shall name him Jesus. He will be great and will be called Son of the Most High, and the Lord God will give him the throne of David his father, and he will rule over the house of Jacob forever, and of his kingdom there will be no end."

LUKE 1:26–33

PRAYER

God of promise and great things to come, you reward the faithful with your loving generosity. In this season of new life, direct our gaze to the wonders around us—the birth of a baby, the giving of food and clothing from one stranger to another, the encouragement and support of friends and family, and the peace, wisdom, and fidelity our Creator showers upon us in abundance. Move my heart, O Lord, to share the love you and I share together. Let my "yes" to you impact not only me but those around me. May family and friends, strangers, and those born on this day hear the echo of my "yes" to you and may your will be done through me, your willing instrument. Amen.

ADVENT ACTION

It can be frustrating at times when we encounter the world on a streak of negativity; it's as if everyone we meet is in a bad mood or, worse, actually trying to put us in a sour, negative mood. But have you ever seen the power of "yes" when it encounters a hardhearted soul? The result is not always the same, but it is interesting from a scientific, sociological point of view. So let's be scientists today.

Encounter a grouch and give him a smile. Say, "God bless you" to someone who's sneezed. Compliment a cashier by maybe saying, "You have a very nice smile." Wish a frowner a great day. Kindness can be contagious. Love can be something that catches on, something with which you "infect" the world. You can begin the ripple effect right now.

Day

13

Mary Is at the Center of the Assembly of Saints

*I*n the Eucharist, we in fact encounter the living Jesus and his strength, and through him we enter into communion with our brothers and sisters in the faith: those who live with us here on earth and those who have gone before us into the next life, the unending life....In the great assembly of saints, God wanted to reserve the first place for the Mother of Jesus. Mary is at the [center] of the communion of saints, as the singular custodian of the bond between the universal Church and Christ, of the bond of the family. She is Mother, She is our Mother, our Mother. For those who want to follow Jesus on the path of the Gospel, she is a trusted guide because she is the first disciple. She is an attentive and caring Mother, to whom we can entrust every desire and difficulty.

FRANCIS' ANGELUS, SOLEMNITY OF ALL SAINTS,
ST. PETER'S SQUARE, NOVEMBER 1, 2014

Scripture

On the third day there was a wedding in Cana in Galilee, and the mother of Jesus was there. Jesus and his disciples were also invited to the wedding. When the wine ran short, the mother of Jesus said to him, "They have no wine." [And] Jesus said to her, "Woman, how does your concern affect me? My hour has not yet come." His mother said to the servers, "Do whatever he tells you."

John 2: 1–5

Prayer

Virgin most holy and immaculate,
to you, the honour of our people,
and the loving protector of our city,
do we turn with loving trust.
You are all-beautiful, O Mary!
In you there is no sin.
Awaken in all of us a renewed desire for holiness:
May the splendour of truth shine forth in our words,
the song of charity resound in our works,
purity and chastity abide in our hearts and bodies,
and the full beauty of the Gospel be evident in our lives....
Amen.

EXCERPTED FROM FRANCIS' PRAYER TO MARY IMMACULATE,
SOLEMNITY OF THE IMMACULATE CONCEPTION
OF THE BLESSED VIRGIN MARY,
DECEMBER 8, 2013

ADVENT ACTION

There are two points to consider today, the first of which has to do with Mary as the center of the communion of saints. Ask yourself: How often do I pray through Mary as an intercessor to my Lord and Savior, Jesus? We can pray through many saints to intercede on our behalf with the Lord, but there is none so close to him as his Mother, who interceded on behalf of a newly married couple asking Jesus to perform the first miracle of his public ministry. Secondly, as we read above, the Holy Father comments on the "wondrous union" that takes place between heaven and earth during the Eucharist. The next time you are at Mass, focus intently on the words of the Eucharistic Prayer. Listen carefully to each word and reflect on the simple beauty and profound mystery of what is being spoken by the priest during this wondrous prayer. Reflect upon the reality of how heaven and earth come together throughout the structure of this wonderful prayer.

Day
14

Heed the Voice of the Poor

*I*n today's world, voices are being raised which we cannot ignore and which implore our Churches to live deeply our identity as disciples of the Lord Jesus Christ.

The first of these voices is that of the poor....We cannot remain indifferent before the cries of our brothers and sisters. These ask of us not only material assistance—needed in so many circumstances—but above all, our help to defend their dignity as human persons, so that they can find the spiritual energy to become once again protagonists in their own lives.

HOMILY ON THE OCCASION OF FRANCIS' APOSTOLIC JOURNEY
TO TURKEY, PATRIARCHAL CHURCH OF ST. GEORGE, ISTANBUL,
NOVEMBER 30, 2014

SCRIPTURE

The way we came to know love was that he laid down his life for us; so we ought to lay down our lives for our brothers. If someone who has worldly means sees a brother in need and refuses him compassion, how can the love of God remain in him? Children, let us love not in word or speech but in deed and truth.

1 JOHN 3:16–18

PRAYER

Dear Father, we are told through your Son, the Word, to "love one another just as he commanded us." Lord, in your wisdom, grace us with the virtues Jesus modeled when he suffered and died for us, loving us to the extent that he laid down his very life for our salvation, that we might inherit his kingdom and be by his side in intimate friendship for all eternity. We are called to love one another with this same passion, to see the face of Jesus in everyone we meet and to respond to their presence in the spirit of his love. What does justice demand from us when we encounter someone lacking basic needs? It demands that we give as Christ gave. May we share your love, Lord, with everyone we encounter, no exceptions. Amen.

ADVENT ACTION

How much do issues of social justice—both in your home country as well as worldwide—demand your attention on a daily basis? Do you consider these issues at all, be they local, regional, national, or international? Based on the message of the Gospels, as modeled through the example of Jesus, how do you respond to the basic needs of people who cry out for justice? Some believers tithe, others give generously of their goods, still others give their time to local food kitchens, demonstrating or protesting peaceably at rallies, or traveling to foreign countries to engage injustice on its home turf. Others commit such issues to prayer.

Pay attention to the injustices in our world—from local to worldwide—and see what engages you to the deepest areas of your conscience. Then discern: how do I go about getting myself involved in this issue that calls out to me so powerfully?

Day
15

Strip Away All That Is Unnecessary

e are all called to be poor, to strip us of ourselves; and to do this we must learn how to be with the poor, to share with those who lack basic necessities, to touch the flesh of Christ! The Christian is not one who speaks about the poor, no! He is one who encounters them, who looks them in the eye, who touches them.... [The Church] must strip away every kind of worldly spirit, which is a temptation for everyone; strip away every action that is not for God, that is not from God; strip away the fear of opening the doors and going out to encounter all, especially the poorest of the poor, the needy, the remote, without waiting.

<small>Francis' Pastoral Visit to Assisi, Meeting with Poor Assisted by Caritas, Room of Renunciation of the Archbishop's Residence, Assisi, October 4, 2013</small>

SCRIPTURE

Blessed are you when they insult you and persecute you and utter every kind of evil against you [falsely] because of me. Rejoice and be glad, for your reward will be great in heaven. Thus they persecuted the prophets who were before you.

MATTHEW 5:11–12

PRAYER

Lord, make me an instrument of thy peace.

Where there is hatred, let me sow love;

Where there is injury, pardon;

Where there is doubt, faith;

Where there is despair, hope;

Where there is darkness, light;

Where there is sadness, joy.

O divine Master, grant that I may not so much seek

To be consoled as to console,

To be understood as to understand,

To be loved as to love;

For it is in giving that we receive;

It is in pardoning that we are pardoned;

It is in dying to self that we are born to eternal life.

THE PRAYER OF ST. FRANCIS

ADVENT ACTION

Over the next several days focus on making Christ the center of your life. For today, contemplate the simple beauty and elegant truths of the Beatitudes (today's Scripture) and the Prayer of St. Francis (today's prayer). What depths these words reach! What fallacies they expose! Ask yourself: what nonessentials do I cling to in my daily life? What baggage and past hurts do I carry with me in my relationships with others? What message is God calling me to share with others that I am reluctant (or perhaps afraid) to share? What is holding me back from saying and doing what I truly feel called to say and do for another?

Open yourself to God on this day, and clear a space at your center for the presence, peace, and passion of Jesus.

Day

16

Christ Is the Center of Creation

The apostle Paul...offers us a profound vision of the centrality of Jesus. He presents Christ to us as the firstborn of all creation: in him, through him and for him all things were created. He is the center of all things, he is the beginning: Jesus Christ, the Lord. God has given him the fullness, the totality, so that in him all things might be reconciled (see Colossians 1:12–20). He is the Lord of creation, he is the Lord of reconciliation.

This image enables to see that Jesus is the center of creation; and so the attitude demanded of us as true believers is that of recognizing and accepting in our lives the centrality of Jesus Christ, in our thoughts, in our words and in our works. And so our thoughts will be *Christian* thoughts, thoughts of Christ. Our works will be *Christian* works, works of Christ; and our words will be *Christian* words, words of Christ.

Francis' Homily at Holy Mass for the Conclusion of the Year of Faith on the Solemnity of Our Lord Jesus Christ, King of the Universe, St. Peter's Square, November 24, 2013

SCRIPTURE

He is the head of the body, the church.
He is the beginning, the firstborn from the dead,
that in all things he himself might be preeminent.
For in him all the fullness was pleased to dwell,
and through him to reconcile all things for him,
making peace by the blood of his cross
[through him], whether those on earth or those in heaven.

COLOSSIANS 1:18–20

PRAYER

Center of our heart, loving Jesus, we invite you inside of us, at our very core, to our very center. We ask that your grace enter us, leaving no room for anything less than what is you, all-goodness, all-knowing, all-loving you. Enter our hearts, Jesus, you who are "the image of the invisible God, the firstborn of all creation." You have reconciled mankind with God by the blood of your cross, we know that when you dwell at our center, we cannot fail, we cannot choose less than the ultimate good nor side with less than the pinnacle of truth. Be with us on this day and every day, guide us and grace us with every good thing according to your will. Amen.

ADVENT ACTION

Has there been a distraction in your life lately? Has there been something or someone casting a shadow on what should be at the center of your life during this Advent season? Does your mind fill with thoughts of anxiety out of the blue?

Try a simple centering prayer. Find ten minutes of quiet time for your own, choose a "sacred word" ("Jesus," "Peace," "Spirit," "Love," "Surrender," "Openness," "Father," and so on), and keep your mind focused on that word. Should any other thoughts creep in, simply return to the word you have chosen as an invitation to God's will and intention for your life. Allow God to work in the silence. If you enjoy the experience, practice this centering prayer style throughout the Advent and Christmas season.

Day
17

Christ Is the Center of the People of God

Besides being the center of creation and the center of reconciliation, Christ is the center of the people of God. Today, he is here in our midst. He is here right now in his word, and he will be here on the altar, alive and present amid us, his people....

Christ, the descendant of King David, is really the "brother" around whom God's people come together. It is he who cares for his people, for all of us, even at the price of his life. In him we are all one, one people, united with him and sharing a single journey, a single destiny. Only in him, in him as the center, do we receive our identity as a people.

FRANCIS' HOMILY AT HOLY MASS FOR THE CONCLUSION OF THE YEAR
OF FAITH ON THE SOLEMNITY OF OUR LORD JESUS CHRIST,
KING OF THE UNIVERSE, ST. PETER'S SQUARE,
NOVEMBER 24, 2013

SCRIPTURE

When Jesus went into the region of Caesarea Philippi he asked his disciples, "Who do people say that the Son of Man is?" They replied, "Some say John the Baptist, others Elijah, still others Jeremiah or one of the prophets." He said to them, "But who do you say that I am?" Simon Peter said in reply, "You are the Messiah, the Son of the living God." Jesus said to him in reply, "Blessed are you, Simon son of Jonah. For flesh and blood has not revealed this to you, but my heavenly Father. And so I say to you, you are Peter, and upon this rock I will build my church, and the gates of the netherworld shall not prevail against it."

MATTHEW 16:13–18

PRAYER

Lord Jesus, my most intimate friend who knows me better than I know myself, may you always be at the center of my heart. When you walked the earth during your three-year public ministry, many people you met did not know what to make of you. Just as you are today, and have always been, you are a healer, a reconciler of division, the Word, the Prince of Peace, the Son of Man, and—as voiced so clearly by the Church's first Holy Father—"the Messiah, the Son of the living God." Be always at my side, dear friend, and more than that may I center my life upon you. Amen.

ADVENT ACTION

Today you'll need a piece of paper and a pen or pencil. Take ten minutes to write a letter to your closest friend, Jesus. Perhaps you could begin by stating how you're feeling on this day. If you're feeling anxious or down, invite him to rest at the center of your heart and bring you peace. If you're feeling terrific and at peace, perhaps you might express your gratitude. List other qualities you appreciate about this friendship; tell Jesus why you make such an effort to put him at the center of your life. Explain why, at times, you lose focus and center on lesser things. As your friend, he will understand the frailty by which we often operate. He knows we stumble and fall. He wants to be as close as possible to us so that, when we do fall, he is there to help us to our feet.

Day
18

Christ Is the Center of History and Every Individual

*F*inally, Christ is the center of the history of humanity and also the center of the history of every individual. To him we can bring the joys and the hopes, the sorrows and troubles which are part of our lives. When Jesus is the center, light shines even amid the darkest times of our lives.

....Each of us has his or her own history: we think of our mistakes, our sins, our good times and our bleak times. We would do well, each one of us, on this day, to think about our own personal history, to look at Jesus and to keep telling him, sincerely and quietly: "Remember me, Lord, now that you are in your kingdom! Jesus, remember me, because I want to be good, but I just don't have the strength: I am a sinner, I am a sinner. But remember me, Jesus! You can remember me because you are at the center, you are truly in your kingdom!" How beautiful this is! Let us all do this today, each one of us in his or her own heart, again and again.

FRANCIS' HOMILY AT HOLY MASS FOR THE CONCLUSION OF THE YEAR OF FAITH ON THE SOLEMNITY OF OUR LORD JESUS CHRIST, KING OF THE UNIVERSE, ST. PETER'S SQUARE, NOVEMBER 24, 2013

SCRIPTURE

Jesus answered, "Amen, amen, I say to you, no one can enter the kingdom of God without being born of water and Spirit. What is born of flesh is flesh and what is born of spirit is spirit. Do not be amazed that I told you, 'You must be born from above.' The wind blows where it wills, and you can hear the sound it makes, but you do not know where it comes from or where it goes; so it is with everyone who is born of the Spirit."

JOHN 3:5–8

PRAYER

Jesus, my rock and my foundation, although my life has had many unexpected twists and turns I thank you and praise you for centering me when I was frightened of losing my way. Although there have been times when I have tried to take the reins myself and everything seemed to be going out of control, I have learned that focusing on you in the midst of the storm is the wisest path to take. And yet from time to time this simple truth seems to elude me and I find myself wandering from the flock. You are the God of second chances (and third, and fourth…) and you are patient with me, always ready to take my hand when I reach for you. I praise your name on this day, and I sing your glory to the ends of the earth. Amen.

ADVENT ACTION

Recall a time in your life when things seemed to be spinning out of control, a time when they surely would have if you had not reached out for your friend Jesus and centered your gaze on him. Call to mind the specifics of the situation: What choices had you made with your mind and heart focused on your own will and not that of the Lord? What moved you to go your own way along this path? What brought you back to the Lord, your most intimate friend, Jesus? What was it about the situation that brought him back to the center, with a full reliance and trust in him and his will for your life? Reflect on this memory and offer it up in praise and thanksgiving to the Lord.

Day

19

Without God at Our Center, We Are Lost

Idols exist, we begin to see, as a pretext for setting ourselves at the center of reality and worshiping the work of our own hands. Once man has lost the fundamental orientation which unifies his existence, he breaks down into the multiplicity of his desires; in refusing to await the time of promise, his life story disintegrates into a myriad of unconnected instants. Idolatry, then, is always polytheism, an aimless passing from one lord to another. Idolatry does not offer a journey but rather a plethora of paths leading nowhere and forming a vast labyrinth. Those who choose not to put their trust in God must hear the din of countless idols crying out: "Put your trust in me!" Faith, tied as it is to conversion, is the opposite of idolatry; it breaks with idols to turn to the living God in a personal encounter.

FRANCIS' ENCYCLICAL LETTER *LUMEN FIDEI*, 13,
JUNE 29, 2013

Scripture

Put to death, then, the parts of you that are earthly: immorality, impurity, passion, evil desire, and the greed that is idolatry. Because of these the wrath of God is coming [upon the disobedient]. By these you too once conducted yourselves, when you lived in that way. But now you must put them all away: anger, fury, malice, slander, and obscene language out of your mouths. Stop lying to one another, since you have taken off the old self with its practices and have put on the new self, which is being renewed, for knowledge, in the image of its creator. Here there is not Greek and Jew, circumcision and uncircumcision, barbarian, Scythian, slave, free; but Christ is all and in all.

COLOSSIANS 3:5–11

Prayer

Great and loving God, you who knows exactly what we need and what does us no good, keep us straight on the path of virtue. Grace us with the pain one feels when one chooses less than you, the pain that reminds us we have pursued idols/ vices that are false gods that glimmer with a deceitful light. Remind us that idolatry leads us nowhere and that we lose our souls in that pursuit. Hold us close to your side, transform and renew us as only you can do when we entrust our faith to your fidelity. When we choose your way, O Lord, we feel only "heartfelt compassion, kindness, humility, gentleness, and patience, bearing with one another and forgiving one another." Amen.

Advent Action

The scriptural passage for today doesn't just instruct us what to put away, it goes on to inform us to put on certain qualities and respond to our neighbors in specific ways: "Put on then...heartfelt compassion, kindness, humility, gentleness, and patience, bearing with one another and forgiving one another, if one has a grievance against another; as the Lord has forgiven you, so must you also do" (Colossians 3:12–13). Meditate on those qualities we are called to put on listed in the scriptural passage above. Read over them several times; notice at which words or qualities your eyes pause. Pray on one or more of these qualities you sometimes find lacking in your life. Pray for God's grace to strengthen you with these abilities. Be specific in the day-to-day situations during which you struggle to showcase these qualities.

Day

20

A Child Changes Your Life

*Y*ou have come with the most beautiful fruit of your love. Motherhood and fatherhood are a gift of God, but to accept the gift, to be astounded by its beauty and to make it shine in society, this is your task. Each of your children is a unique creature that will never be duplicated in the history of humanity. When one understands this, or that God wanted each one, we are astounded by how great a miracle a child is! A child changes your life! We have all seen—men, women—that when a child arrives, life changes, it is another thing. A son or daughter is a miracle that changes life. You, boys and girls, are exactly this: each one of you is the unique fruit of love, you come from love and you grow in love. You are unique, but not alone!

FRANCIS' ADDRESS TO THE NATIONAL NUMEROUS FAMILY ASSOCIATION,
PAUL VI AUDIENCE HALL,
DECEMBER 28, 2014

Scripture

Each year his parents went to Jerusalem for the feast of Passover, and when he was twelve years old, they went up according to festival custom. After they had completed its days, as they were returning, the boy Jesus remained behind in Jerusalem, but his parents did not know it. Thinking that he was in the caravan, they journeyed for a day and looked for him among their relatives and acquaintances, but not finding him, they returned to Jerusalem to look for him. After three days they found him in the temple, sitting in the midst of the teachers, listening to them and asking them questions, and all who heard him were astounded at his understanding and his answers.

LUKE 2:41–47

Prayer

Good and loving Father, your Child changed the world like no other. Through the mystery of the Incarnation he reunited Creator and mankind, healing the rift caused by Adam's sin. Children continue to change the world, though on a smaller scale. When a new child enters the lives of his parents, their focus turns from one another to what they have created in love and in partnership with your love. Every child is unique and special, adding something wonderful to creation and bringing something new—a deeper understanding of love— to his or her mother and father. As the Father loves the Son, may we love each and all our children, seeing them as unique, as wonderful, and as the miracle that they are. Amen.

ADVENT ACTION

Are you aware of a new child born into the life of a family member, friend, or parishioner these last few months? If you are a parent yourself, you can understand what these new parents are experiencing in their first days as caregivers to this child. There is joy, surprise, anxiety, frustration, and myriad more emotions that accompany the welcoming of a new life into a home.

Set aside a period of time during your prayers these next few days and remember these parents and their new child. Pray that the child experiences comfort and ease as he or she adapts to life at home. Pray that the parents experience peace and wonder at the new life that has entered their home. Pray that these parents experience every wondrous joy and surprise possible as their love for God deepens during their roles as mother and father.

Day
21

Pass on the Faith

*Y*ou, children and young people, are the fruit of the tree that is the family: you are good fruit when the tree has deep roots—your grandparents—and a strong trunk—your parents. Jesus said that every sound tree bears good fruit but every bad tree bears evil fruit. The great human family is like a forest, where sound trees bear solidarity, communion, trust, support, security, happy sobriety, friendship. The presence of large families is a hope for society.

FRANCIS' ADDRESS TO THE NATIONAL NUMEROUS FAMILY ASSOCIATION,
PAUL VI AUDIENCE HALL,
DECEMBER 28, 2014

SCRIPTURE

People were bringing even infants to him that he might touch them, and when the disciples saw this, they rebuked them. Jesus, however, called the children to himself and said, "Let the children come to me and do not prevent them; for the kingdom of God belongs to such as these. Amen, I say to you, whoever does not accept the kingdom of God like a child will not enter it."

LUKE 18:15–17

Prayer

Lord and Teacher, model of humility and mercy, you showed us the way to the Father in everything you did and said, providing for us the perfect example to imitate and emulate in our daily lives. Grace us with the virtues necessary to mirror your love so that everyone, especially children, will know your love by our words and deeds. We ask that you never allow our sins to corrupt the young and the innocent; we ask that we—as instruments of your peace—be moved by your love to the point that others know your love through us and be drawn to you. Let us praise your name to the generations that follow us on earth, and may we do this in a spirit of gratitude, enthusiasm, wonder, generosity, fortitude, and charity that knows only you as its source. Amen.

Advent Action

Reflect for ten to fifteen minutes today on the children who are a part of your life. Perhaps you see these children daily, every other week or month, annually, or just during the holidays. How do you model Christ to them? Are they able to see God's love operating through your words and actions? How do you connect with them? Do you engage them in discussions about what interests them? Can you help them to see how God is working through them in everything they do? Pray that God might help you view the world through the eyes of a child so you might better relate to these young people.

Day

22

God's Gift of Love Transforms Us

*T*oday I would like to reflect with you on the Birth of Jesus, the feast of trust and of hope which overcomes uncertainty and pessimism. And the reason for our hope is this: God is with us and God still trusts us! ....

Hence the great "gift" of the Child of Bethlehem: He brings us a spiritual energy, an energy which helps us not to despair in our struggle, in our hopelessness, in our sadness, for it is an energy that warms and transforms the heart. Indeed, the Birth of Jesus brings us the good news that we are loved immensely and uniquely by God, and he not only enables us to know this love, he also gives it to us, he communicates it to us!

FRANCIS, GENERAL AUDIENCE, ST. PETER'S SQUARE,
DECEMBER 18, 2013

Scripture

Now you are Christ's body, and individually parts of it. Some people God has designated in the church to be, first, apostles; second, prophets; third, teachers; then, mighty deeds; then, gifts of healing, assistance, administration, and varieties of tongues. Are all apostles? Are all prophets? Are all teachers? Do all work mighty deeds? Do all have gifts of healing? Do all speak in tongues? Do all interpret?

1 Corinthians 12:27–30

Prayer

Lord God, you dwell in my heart and direct my course when I seek that your will be done through me, your willing instrument. I pray that I seek only to do your will through the many gifts you have given me. I know I am special and I am your unique creation, made in your image, but I am also aware that I am a smaller part of a larger body, Christ's body on earth. I am called to a form of service for which I have been specifically made and I am here to tell you that I am excited and committed to serve according to your will. You have pitched your tent with us, as the Holy Father states. I know you are beside me in all that I do in your name, and within me whenever I speak your word. Amen.

ADVENT ACTION

Make a list today of the gifts you've been given by the Spirit. Perhaps some of these gifts come easily—almost second nature—and others you've worked hard to develop. These gifts could range from being compassionate to speaking well to exuding kindness to being a good listener to not stooping to gossip. Whatever you view as a gift, include it on your list. After you've made this list, write a sentence or two after each gift you've listed and expand on how using that gift attracts others to God's love. How does it model the love Christ modeled for us during his earthly ministry? In what ways are you drawn to God when you exercise the gifts he has given you as a member of Christ's body?

Day

23

Our Souls Call Out for the Lord

The Lord comes twice. His first coming is what we are about to commemorate, his physical birth. Then, he will come at the end of time, at the close of history. However, St. Bernard tells us that there is a third coming of the Lord: his coming to us each day. Each day, the Lord visits his Church. He visits each one of us....

Therefore, our souls are waiting in anticipation for the coming of the Lord, open souls calling out: "Come, Lord!" Over the course of these days, the Holy Spirit moves in the heart of each one of us, forming this prayer within us: "come, come!" Throughout the Advent Season the Church keeps watch like Mary. And watching is the virtue, the attitude, of pilgrims. We are pilgrims. Are we watching or are we closed? Are we vigilant or are we safe and secure in an inn, no longer wanting to continue on? Are we pilgrims or are we wandering?

FRANCIS' MORNING MEDITATION "AWAITING THE BIRTH,"
CHAPEL OF THE *DOMUS SANCTAE MARTHAE,*
DECEMBER 23, 2013

SCRIPTURE

"[T]he bridegroom came and those who were ready went into the wedding feast with him. Then the door was locked. Afterwards the other virgins came and said, 'Lord, Lord, open the door for us!' But he said in reply, 'Amen, I say to you, I do not know you.' Therefore, stay awake, for you know neither the day nor the hour."

MATTHEW 25:10–13

PRAYER

Kind and loving God, you are with us always; may we be aware of your constant presence and may we accept every moment in our lives as an opportunity to meet you in prayer. Though our lives continue to take us where they will, may this path be according to your will. May we see every encounter with another, every moment of quiet, and every task we attend to as a chance to know you ever deeper, with greater intimacy than before. May we be alert to your presence, to your daily arrival, as the wise virgins from today's Scripture; and may we trust in you as we live our pilgrim lives in anticipation of your Second Coming at the end of time. Amen.

ADVENT ACTION

Saint Thérèse of Lisieux, a doctor of the Church, developed a way of life called the Little Way, a prayer method through which her every thought, word, and action became a prayer offering to God. While in the convent, Thérèse was assigned some mundane and undesirable tasks—washing clothes, cleaning the floor, caring for an ill-tempered and elderly fellow sister. Thérèse approached her every act and duty as a prayer to God, offering up her service in praise of his name, and seeing God's presence in every little thing she did so that she might grow ever closer to him in intimate friendship.

How does your life change when you see God present in every small task you do? With the approach of the Little Way, every aspect of our life is immersed in God, and every breath we take is a prayer.

Day

24

Receive the Lord With an Open Soul

The Church invites us to pray "come!" and to "open our souls in watchfulness." We are invited to perceive and understand "what is happening within us," to ask "if the Lord comes or does not come; if there is room for the Lord, or if there is room for celebration, for shopping, for making noise." This examination of conscience should lead us to ask ourselves: "Are our souls open, as the soul of Holy Mother Church is open, and as Mary's soul was open? Or have we closed our souls and put a highly erudite note on the door saying: please do not disturb?

FRANCIS' MORNING MEDITATION "AWAITING THE BIRTH,"
CHAPEL OF THE *DOMUS SANCTAE MARTHAE*,
DECEMBER 23, 2013

Scripture

[Simeon] was righteous and devout, awaiting the consolation of Israel, and the holy Spirit was upon him. It had been revealed to him by the holy Spirit that he should not see death before he had seen the Messiah of the Lord. He came in the Spirit into the temple; and when the parents brought in the child Jesus to perform the custom of the law in regard to him, he took him into his arms and blessed God, saying:

"Now, Master, you may let your servant go
  in peace, according to your word,
for my eyes have seen your salvation,
  which you prepared in sight of all the peoples,
a light for revelation to the Gentiles,
  and glory for your people Israel."

LUKE 2:25–32

Prayer

Lord God, your will is what I need. You know my needs before I have an inkling of what they might be. This is where faith and trust must enter my heart. I must trust you more than I trust myself. This truth frightens me. You are there to put my mind at ease and my heart at peace. There is great beauty and innocence in the Christ Child, but there is a wonderful opportunity and challenge upon his arrival. He sanctified us by his Incarnation, and he defeated sin and made possible our salvation by his death and resurrection. Our challenge is to ask to participate in this salvation that we might know our Savior for all eternity following our life on earth. Amen.

ADVENT ACTION

When did you last write a poem? Elementary school? High school? Never? Today, with pen and paper, give it a shot. It doesn't need to be lengthy. Imagine Mary's anticipation as her pregnancy progressed toward delivery in Bethlehem. Then imagine the righteous and devout Simeon from today's Scripture passage. Think about the waiting he had to do. Consider his patience during his long period of anticipating the arrival of the Savior.

Today voice your anticipation in verse. It doesn't have to rhyme, but it can. Allow the Christ Child's impending arrival to inspire your thoughts and words. Let excitement and wonder flow through you as you await God becoming man and every wondrous reality that accompanies this marvelous mystery.

Day

25

We Wait With Great Anticipation

Come, Lord! In [these] final [days] before Christmas the Church repeats the prayer, "Come, Lord!" and she calls out to the Lord with various and different names: O Wisdom, O Root of Jesse, O Dayspring, O King of the Nations, and today, O Emmanuel.

The Church calls out to the Lord in this way because she is awaiting a birth. This week the Church is like Mary: she is awaiting a birth. The Virgin sensed within herself, in body and in soul, that the birth of her child was near. Surely in her heart she said to the baby she was carrying in her womb: "Come, I want to see your face, for they have told me you will be great!"

FRANCIS' MORNING MEDITATION "AWAITING THE BIRTH,"
CHAPEL OF THE *DOMUS SANCTAE MARTHAE,*
DECEMBER 23, 2013

SCRIPTURE

Therefore the Lord himself will give you a sign; the young woman, pregnant and about to bear a son, shall name him Emmanuel.

ISAIAH 7:14

PRAYER

Dear Lord, I can hardly contain myself at your impending arrival. The fact that you love us, your creation, so much that you would unite your divinity with our humanity for the sake of our mutual communion is a reality so wonderful that it almost seems like a dream, due to your unfathomable love. What have we done to deserve this? Nothing. Your love is freely given; it is not earned by us in any way. You loved us into creation and—despite our sinning—you never cease loving us, even to the extent of becoming one of us. May your grace continue to shine upon us and may I express my gratitude in song, word, and action. May your grace move me to live ever closer to your will, and may I behold your beatific vision for all eternity following my passing from this earth. Amen.

ADVENT ACTION

If you are able, get out of the house today and experience the true energy of the Christmas season. Go to Mass, share in the excitement and anticipation of the coming of the Christ Child with a group of believers. If you don't mind crowds, go to the mall and feel the press of humanity upon you, including the exuberant joy of children who can hardly contain themselves. The hustle and bustle of the Christmas season doesn't have to be a negative thing. If its focus is worldliness, then it serves no good purpose. But if it serves as a positive means to express the expectation of the arrival of something truly wondrous, and if it inspires people to give to others as an expression of the love they feel from the great gift of the Father, then perhaps there is value to the hustle and bustle of the holiday season.

Day

26

Fraternity Is the Pathway to Peace

*F*raternity is an essential human quality, for we are relational beings. A lively awareness of our relatedness helps us to look upon and to treat each person as a true sister or brother; without fraternity it is impossible to build a just society and a solid and lasting peace. We should remember that fraternity is generally first learned in the family, thanks above all to the responsible and complementary roles of each of its members, particularly the father and the mother. The family is the wellspring of all fraternity, and as such it is the foundation and the first pathway to peace, since, by its vocation, it is meant to spread its love to the world around it.

FRANCIS' MESSAGE
"FRATERNITY, THE FOUNDATION AND PATHWAY TO PEACE"
FOR THE CELEBRATION OF WORLD DAY OF PEACE,
JANUARY 1, 2014

SCRIPTURE

While [Joseph and Mary] were [in Bethlehem], the time came
for her to have her child, and she gave birth to her firstborn
son. She wrapped him in swaddling clothes and laid him in a
manger, because there was no room for them in the inn.

LUKE 2:6–7

PRAYER

God of peace, you know well our world suffers from a
stunning absence of peace. Race against race, religion against
religion, haves against have-nots, anxieties and anger raging
within people—the fighting seems unceasing. Prayers for
peace in our world seem to be in vain, too weak to impact
the hurts, angers, and acts of vengeance and retaliation that
span thousands of years. Yet, on Christmas Day the Prince
of Peace was born into our world. He, of course, was not
brought into a world of peace, but what he made possible
through the great mystery of the Incarnation was the reality
that the kingdom of God could be built on earth. Peace on
earth, no longer a dream, was now something to be realized.
God of love, help us realize this peace in our lives. Amen.

ADVENT ACTION

As the hustle and bustle of the Advent season—and all of its accompanying errands—comes to a close, all we need seek is the peace our Lord provides, the peace he offers to us every moment of the day if only we turn our attention to it. The commercialism of the season is easy and fun to get wrapped up in, but where we set our priorities is our choice. Even in the midst of a crowded mall or high-traffic road, we can choose to enter into the peace our Lord provides. The next time you find yourself in a stressful situation—in a large crowd with people pressing upon you or in the middle of a traffic jam—call upon the peace that God offers; it's there waiting for you. God came so we might be saved and know the eternal peace he offers, a peace we can share with him any time in our daily lives.

Day

27

The Lord Works in Silence

Mary "was silent, but within her heart how many things she said to the Lord" in that crucial moment in history. Likely, Mary would have thought back to the angel's words regarding her Son: "On that day you told me he would be great! You told me he would be given the throne of David his father and that he would reign forever! But now look there" at the Cross. Mary, Pope Francis added, "veiled in silence the mystery which she did not understand. And through silence she allowed the mystery to grow and flourish," thus bringing great hope to all.

FRANCIS' MORNING MEDITATION "MYSTERY DOESN'T SEEK PUBLICITY,"
CHAPEL OF THE *DOMUS SANCTAE MARTHAE,*
DECEMBER 20, 2013

Scripture

When the angels went away from them to heaven, the shepherds said to one another, "Let us go, then, to Bethlehem to see this thing that has taken place, which the Lord has made known to us." So they went in haste and found Mary and Joseph, and the infant lying in the manger. When they saw this, they made known the message that had been told them about this child. All who heard it were amazed by what had been told them by the shepherds. And Mary kept all these things, reflecting on them in her heart.

LUKE 2:15–19

Prayer

Mysterious God, who has revealed himself to us throughout history and in relationship with each of us throughout our lives, quiet our busy minds and restless hearts at this time and move us to embrace the silence in which we can hear that still, small voice. Your calling for each of us is a unique invitation to know you in an intimate relationship. We are called to express your love for humanity. It is in silence that you reveal this mystery to us, and we are wise to look upon Mary as our ideal. Grace us with this faculty to embrace silence in our faith, that our friendship with the divine will deepen as he reveals his mystery to us in quiet. Amen.

ADVENT ACTION

What role does silence play in your life? Silence makes some people uncomfortable. The need for the distraction of noise—the television or radio on in the background, always needing to be on the phone—is too enticing for those people who cannot abide silence. Perhaps for some people, silence is nearly impossible to find. We care for kids, run errands, and work, so experiencing quiet for ten straight minutes is a daily challenge.

Today, *make* time for silence. Make it God's time. Usher the children from the room, silence the television and radio, and create a still, quiet space for God. Let the Father speak to you in this silence in the same manner he approached Mary and Joseph. Make quiet your space. Embrace it as a place wherein God has complete access to you and you to him. You will not miss one word he has for you and you will be able to embrace his will without distraction.

Day

28

We Entrust Ourselves to the Virgin Mary

Our thoughts turn to Mary Most Holy, who, here in Bethlehem, gave birth to Jesus her Son. Our Lady is the one who, more than any other person, contemplated God in the human face of Jesus. Assisted by Saint Joseph, she wrapped him in swaddling clothes and laid him in the manger.

Mary, watch over our families, our young people and our elderly. Watch over those who have lost faith and hope. Comfort the sick, the imprisoned and all who suffer. Watch over the Church's Pastors and the entire community of believers; may they may be "salt and light" in this blessed land.

FRANCIS, *REGINA CAELI*, PILGRIMAGE TO THE HOLY LAND
ON THE OCCASION OF THE FIFTIETH ANNIVERSARY OF THE MEETING
BETWEEN POPE PAUL VI AND PATRIARCH ATHENAGORAS IN JERUSALEM,
MAY 25, 2014

Scripture

Such was his intention when, behold, the angel of the Lord appeared to him in a dream and said, "Joseph, son of David, do not be afraid to take Mary your wife into your home. For it is through the holy Spirit that this child has been conceived in her. She will bear a son and you are to name him Jesus, because he will save his people from their sins." All this took place to fulfill what the Lord had said through the prophet:

"Behold, the virgin shall be with child and bear a son,
  and they shall name him Emmanuel,"
which means "God is with us."

MATTHEW 1:20–23

Prayer

Great and loving Father, today we pray for the intercession of the Blessed Virgin Mary and St. Joseph, her loving spouse and the stepfather of Jesus, that they may intercede with you on our behalf. Mary and Joseph, pray for us that we may be graced with the courage and strength to say "yes" to the will of God, whatever he may ask. In the midst of uncertainty, fear, and danger, you said "yes" and embraced the will of the Father—without counting the cost—and fulfilled your role in God's plan for our salvation. Pray for us that we might have this confidence in God, that our "yes" may be spoken with full faith and courage. Amen.

ADVENT ACTION

Consider the stresses, joys, surprises, trials, and tribulations of the Holy Family. From the time of the annunciation through their lives in Nazareth to the death and resurrection of Jesus to the assumption of the Blessed Virgin. Now consider your own family's stresses, joys, trials, and tribulations. How has your family come together during difficult times to support one another? How have you come together to celebrate joyous moments? Can you see the Holy Family as a model for your own, with faith in the will of our heavenly Father as its core? In what ways has your family been faithful to the call of the Father? How has this faith life united your family?

How can you and your family further model yourselves according to the spirit of the Holy Family? Perhaps you can discuss this during a dinner conversation or in family prayer.

PART II

~~~

READINGS *for the* TWELVE DAYS *of* CHRISTMAS

Day

29

What an Impact One Family Can Have!

The evangelist Luke tells us that the Blessed Mother and Saint Joseph, in keeping with the Law of Moses, took the Baby Jesus to the temple to offer him to the Lord, and that an elderly man and woman, Simeon and Anna, moved by the Holy Spirit, went to meet them and acknowledged Jesus as the Messiah (see Luke 2:22–38). Simeon took him in his arms and thanked God that he had finally "seen" salvation. Anna, despite her advanced age, found new vigour and began to speak to everyone about the Baby. It is a beautiful image: two young parents and two elderly people, brought together by Jesus. He is the one who brings together and unites generations! He is the inexhaustible font of that love which overcomes every occasion of self-absorption, solitude, and sadness. In your journey as a family, you share so many beautiful moments: meals, rest, housework, leisure, prayer, trips and pilgrimages, and times of mutual support....Nevertheless, if there is no love then there is no joy, and authentic love comes to us from Jesus.

FRANCIS' LETTER TO FAMILIES,

FEAST OF THE PRESENTATION OF THE LORD,

FEBRUARY 2, 2014

Scripture

The child's father and mother were amazed at what was said about him; and Simeon blessed them and said to Mary his mother, "Behold, this child is destined for the fall and rise of many in Israel, and to be a sign that will be contradicted (and you yourself a sword will pierce) so that the thoughts of many hearts may be revealed." There was also a prophetess, Anna, the daughter of Phanuel, of the tribe of Asher. She was advanced in years, having lived seven years with her husband after her marriage, and then as a widow until she was eighty-four. She never left the temple, but worshiped night and day with fasting and prayer. And coming forward at that very time, she gave thanks to God and spoke about the child to all who were awaiting the redemption of Jerusalem.

LUKE 2:33–38

Prayer

Creative and generous Father, you have given your sons and daughters many talents and abilities to use in building up your kingdom as we labor according to your will. We are told not to keep these gifts to ourselves, like a lamp beneath a bushel basket. We are called to unite with one another as one body, whether our group is a formal family, an association, the parish in its entirety, or the Church on earth as one. We have work to do, sharing these great gifts. May we be graced as formal families, community-outreach groups, and as a parish family to praise your name and build your kingdom. Amen.

CHRISTMAS ACTION

Think on the new year to come. In what way can your family be transformed according to the Holy Spirit to impact your local church? Think creatively. How can the combined efforts of your core family or a parish group help to shine a light on the beauty of the Gospel message? How could you attract more families to the exciting endeavors taking place at your parish? If your goal is to involve your family more in the life of your parish, to what activities would they be receptive? See what your parish has to offer and evaluate the possibilities with your family.

Day
30

We Are Called to Go Forth

The word of God constantly shows us how God challenges those who believe in him "to go forth." Abraham received the call to set out for a new land (see Genesis 12:1–3). Moses heard God's call: "Go, I send you" (Exodus 3:10) and led the people toward the promised land (see Exodus 3:17). To Jeremiah God says: "To all whom I send you, you shall go" (Jeremiah 1:7). In our day Jesus' command to "go and make disciples" echoes in the changing scenarios and ever new challenges to the Church's mission of evangelization, and all of us are called to take part in this new missionary "going forth." Each Christian and every community must discern the path that the Lord points out, but all of us are asked to obey his call to go forth from our own comfort zone in order to reach all the "peripheries" in need of the light of the Gospel.

FRANCIS' APOSTOLIC EXHORTATION *EVANGELII GAUDIUM*, 20,
NOVEMBER 24, 2013

SCRIPTURE

Whatever town or village you enter, look for a worthy person in it, and stay there until you leave. As you enter a house, wish it peace. If the house is worthy, let your peace come upon it; if not, let your peace return to you. Whoever will not receive you or listen to your words—go outside that house or town and shake the dust from your feet.

MATTHEW 10:11–14

PRAYER

Lord Jesus Christ, just as you called your twelve apostles to go forth and make known the peace and Good News of the Gospel, so you call us to go forth and make known your coming and the joy and peace you bring. We do this in part by living lives of happiness, living lives according to your will, filled with the joy and peace of the Spirit. People we meet see this joy and peace within us and want to know how they can live in a like manner. We are called to live lives centered in Christ, focused on faith. Move our hearts to continue in this manner, and may we be living examples of the Gospel message to all we encounter. Amen.

CHRISTMAS ACTION

Today, or the next day you are out and about, be very aware of your words and actions—particularly your actions. Be aware also of your mood. Before you go out from your home, pray that your mood exudes the joy and peace that only Christ can offer. Ask Jesus specifically for this so that everyone you encounter can see the Gospel in action. Words may not even be necessary. Act according to the faith you've been given and the Gospel way of life that has been modeled for you by your most intimate friend. See how people change once you've changed. They see you living the Gospel life, filled with the Spirit, and they will want it, too.

Day

31

All Has Been Revealed

aith's new way of seeing things is centered on Christ. Faith in Christ brings salvation because in him our lives become radically open to a love that precedes us, a love that transforms us from within, acting in us and through us....Christ came down to earth and rose from the dead; by his incarnation and resurrection, the Son of God embraced the whole of human life and history, and now dwells in our hearts through the Holy Spirit. Faith knows that God has drawn close to us, that Christ has been given to us as a great gift which inwardly transforms us, dwells within us and thus bestows on us the light that illumines the origin and the end of life.

FRANCIS' ENCYCLICAL LETTER *LUMEN FIDEI*, 20,
JUNE 29, 2013

SCRIPTURE

We know that all things work for good for those who love God, who are called according to his purpose. For those he foreknew he also predestined to be conformed to the image of his Son, so that he might be the firstborn among many brothers. And those he predestined he also called; and those he called he also justified; and those he justified he also glorified. What then shall we say to this? If God is for us, who can be against us?

ROMANS 8:28–31

PRAYER

Generous and loving Lord, we are saved, invited, encouraged, prodded, and embraced to participate in your salvation. We cannot earn it from you. We are saved through Jesus Christ. Only by his death and resurrection is communion with you possible. Animal sacrifices of old could not unite what had been broken in Eden; it took the mystery of the God-man, it took his sacrifice on the cross, to bridge the gap made by Adam's sin. Only a reality that could be wholly God and wholly man could achieve that reunion. All that is called for on our behalf is faith. Faith: complete trust and confidence in God. And when we are faithful to God, we become Christlike and share in all that he revealed. May the grace and guidance of the Holy Spirit—given to us by the risen Christ at Pentecost—direct our way and may our faith vision always rest on the face of God. Amen.

CHRISTMAS ACTION

Meditate on and/or practice a cardinal virtue during each of the coming four days. Today, pray that the Holy Spirit guides you in your practice of these virtues: prudence, justice, fortitude, and temperance. Briefly reflect on each one; consult a dictionary or the *Catechism* should you need to better understand their basic meanings. "'If anyone loves righteousness, [Wisdom's] labors are virtues; for she teaches temperance and prudence, justice, and courage.' These virtues are praised under other names in many passages of Scripture" (*CCC* 1805).

Day

32

Prudence Guides Our Virtues

We come to see the difference, then, which faith makes for us. Those who believe are transformed by the love to which they have opened their hearts in faith. By their openness to this offer of primordial love, their lives are enlarged and expanded. "It is no longer I who live, but Christ who lives in me" (Galatians 2:20). "May Christ dwell in your hearts through faith" (Ephesians 3:17). The self-awareness of the believer now expands because of the presence of another; it now lives in this other and thus, in love, life takes on a whole new breadth. Here we see the Holy Spirit at work. The Christian can see with the eyes of Jesus and share in his mind, his filial disposition, because he or she shares in his love, which is the Spirit. In the love of Jesus, we receive in a certain way his vision. Without being conformed to him in love, without the presence of the Spirit, it is impossible to confess him as Lord (see 1 Corinthians 12:3).

FRANCIS' ENCYCLICAL LETTER *LUMEN FIDEI*, 21,
JUNE 29, 2013

SCRIPTURE

For this reason I kneel before the Father, from whom every family in heaven and on earth is named, that he may grant you in accord with the riches of his glory to be strengthened with power through his Spirit in the inner self, and that Christ may dwell in your hearts through faith; that you, rooted and grounded in love, may have strength to comprehend with all the holy ones what is the breadth and length and height and depth, and to know the love of Christ that surpasses knowledge, so that you may be filled with all the fullness of God.

EPHESIANS 3:14–19

PRAYER

Lord who knows us better than we know ourselves, you do not ask that we *be* Christ, but that we be *Christlike*. We cannot be perfect, yet we are called to strive to live our lives without sin. We stumble and fall and you put us back on our feet through reconciliation. Lord, you somehow transform our weaknesses into our greatest strengths, especially when we are open about these weaknesses and raise them up to you. May you strengthen these weak parts of our spirit and faith life, may you unite these weakened parts of our person with others who can benefit from these weaknesses by application of their accompanying strengths, and vice versa. Your creativity in blessing your creation knows no bounds. Grace us with the desire for your cardinal virtues, that we might grow ever closer to you in friendship. Amen.

CHRISTMAS ACTION

"Prudence is the virtue that disposes practical reason to discern our true good in every circumstance and to choose the right means of achieving it" (*CCC* 1806).

Take five to ten minutes to reflect on the cardinal virtue of prudence, the charioteer of the virtues: How do you gauge your conscience in judging moral issues? Do you stand firm in your judgment of procreative issues, social justice matters, and so forth? Meditate on the popular moral issues of the day. How does your conscience direct your conduct in these matters?

Day

33

Truth Is the Root of Faith and Justice

We need knowledge, we need truth, because without these we cannot stand firm, we cannot move forward. Faith without truth does not save, it does not provide a sure footing. It remains a beautiful story, the projection of our deep yearning for happiness, something capable of satisfying us to the extent that we are willing to deceive ourselves. Either that, or it is reduced to a lofty sentiment which brings consolation and cheer, yet remains prey to the vagaries of our spirit and the changing seasons, incapable of sustaining a steady journey through life....But precisely because of its intrinsic link to truth, faith is...able to offer a new light....For it sees further into the distance and takes into account the hand of God, who remains faithful to his covenant and his promises.

FRANCIS' ENCYCLICAL LETTER *LUMEN FIDEI*, 24,
JUNE 29, 2013

Scripture

Thus says God, the LORD,
  who created the heavens and stretched them out,
  who spread out the earth and its produce,
Who gives breath to its people
  and spirit to those who walk on it:
I, the LORD, have called you for justice,
  I have grasped you by the hand;
I formed you, and set you
  as a covenant for the people,
  a light for the nations,
To open the eyes of the blind,
  to bring out prisoners from confinement,
  and from the dungeon, those who live in darkness.

ISAIAH 42:5–7

Prayer

Loving God, you honor us with your presence. We enter into relationship with you because you have graced us with the gift of faith. With it, we better understand your truth and what it means to be just. We are called by your glory to give you your due and to give our fellow man and woman his and her due by this same virtue of justice that is fostered within us by the truth we take on as faith, a faith that grows through the indwelling of your Holy Spirit, a justice that seeks to honor and serve another, as we see your Son, our Lord Jesus, within each person. Move us to serve you by serving our brothers and sisters in righteousness. Amen.

CHRISTMAS ACTION

"Justice is the moral virtue that consists in the constant and firm will to give their due to God and neighbor. Justice toward God is called the 'virtue of religion.' Justice toward men disposes one to respect the rights of each and to establish in human relationships the harmony that promotes equity with regard to persons and to the common good" (*CCC* 1807).

Reflect on your relationship with God from the point of view of justice. In what ways do you give God his due? Reflect on your relationship with others. How clearly do you see them as children of God, separate from their worldly status? Contemplate a world in which each person is granted the same dignity and justice regardless of race, gender, or economic status. Pray on this. Imagine how you might facilitate this virtue in your own life.

Day

34

Through Fortitude, Our Bond to the Truth Is Strengthened

Today more than ever, we need to be reminded of this bond between faith and truth, given the crisis of truth in our age. In contemporary culture, we often tend to consider the only real truth to be that of technology: truth is what we succeed in building and measuring by our scientific know-how, truth is what works and what makes life easier and more comfortable. Nowadays this appears as the only truth that is certain....But Truth itself, the truth which would comprehensively explain our life as individuals and in society, is regarded with suspicion. Surely this kind of truth—we hear it said—is what was claimed by the great totalitarian movements of the last century, a truth that imposed its own world view in order to crush the actual lives of individuals. In the end, what we are left with is relativism, in which the question of universal truth—and ultimately this means the question of God—is no longer relevant.

FRANCIS' ENCYCLICAL LETTER *LUMEN FIDEI*, 25,
JUNE 29, 2013

SCRIPTURE

His disciples said, "Now you are talking plainly, and not in any figure of speech. Now we realize that you know everything and that you do not need to have anyone question you. Because of this we believe that you came from God." Jesus answered them, "Do you believe now? Behold, the hour is coming and has arrived when each of you will be scattered to his own home and you will leave me alone. But I am not alone, because the Father is with me. I have told you this so that you might have peace in me. In the world you will have trouble, but take courage, I have conquered the world."

JOHN 16:29–33

PRAYER

Lord Jesus Christ, you know everything that it means to be human: the suffering, the temptations, and the fortitude required to face trials and persecutions. How easy it sometimes feels to respond to hatred with hatred, but with you as our model we can enter into a relationship with you that includes the virtue of fortitude, a way of life that seeks to pursue the good, that strengthens our commitment to resist temptation. Grace us in a special way this day, Lord Jesus, guide us as you walked this earth, keeping your attention constantly on your heavenly Father. Amen.

CHRISTMAS ACTION

"Fortitude is the moral virtue that ensures firmness in difficulties and constancy in the pursuit of the good. It strengthens the resolve to resist temptations and to overcome obstacles in the moral life" (*CCC* 1808).

Sometimes when we are confronted with a life obstacle, a temptation, all we seem to see is the enticement right before our eyes. These are moments when we must catch ourselves and rely on the virtue of fortitude with which God has graced us. Call to mind a temptation that visits you regularly. Reflect on what would happen if—instead of taking hold of that lure right then and there—you paused, evaluated the value of that temptation, and called on God for the grace of fortitude.

Day
35

Temperance Provides Balance

*C*an Christian faith provide a service to the common good with regard to the right way of understanding truth? To answer this question, we need to reflect on the kind of knowledge involved in faith. Here a saying of Saint Paul can help us: "One believes with the heart" (Romans 10:10). In the Bible, the heart is the core of the human person, where all his or her different dimensions intersect: body and spirit, interiority and openness to the world and to others, intellect, will and affectivity. If the heart is capable of holding all these dimensions together, it is because it is where we become open to truth and love, where we let them touch us and deeply transform us.

FRANCIS' ENCYCLICAL LETTER *LUMEN FIDEI*, 26,
JUNE 29, 2013

SCRIPTURE

Do you not know that the runners in the stadium all run in the race, but only one wins the prize? Run so as to win. Every athlete exercises discipline in every way. They do it to win a perishable crown, but we an imperishable one. Thus I do not run aimlessly; I do not fight as if I were shadowboxing. No, I drive my body and train it, for fear that, after having preached to others, I myself should be disqualified.

1 CORINTHIANS 9:24–27

PRAYER

Generous Father, your creation, this earth on which we live and those with whom we share it, was created for our pleasure and the joy of relationship and friendship. You want us to be pleased—to experience pleasure—with your creation, but not to the extent that an imbalance or unhealthiness of desire takes root. Grace us and strengthen us with the virtue of temperance so we might know the goodness of your creation without abusing it or confusing it with the ultimate good—its Creator, you our loving God. May we experience the pleasure of your creation in a manner that only strengthens our bond with you. Amen.

"Temperance is the moral virtue that moderates the attraction of pleasures and provides balance in the use of created goods. It ensures the will's mastery over instincts and keeps desires within the limits of what is honorable. The temperate person directs the sensitive appetites toward what is good and maintains a healthy discretion" (*CCC* 1809).

Take some quiet time today to contemplate the beauty of God's creation; not just the splendor of nature but also what men and women have made of this creation through their God-given ingenuity and the grace of resourcefulness. Consider the potential pitfalls of this created world that tempt you to invest an inordinate amount of your time and attention in what has been created for your pleasure. How do these pitfalls shift your focus away from what is most important: the Creator himself?

Day

36

The Family Fully Alive

The values and virtues of the family, its essential truths, are the strengths on which the family nucleus rests and cannot be called into question. We are called, rather, to review our own lifestyle which is always exposed to the risk of being "contaminated" by a worldly mentality—individualist, consumerist, hedonist—and to rediscover ever again the royal road, in order to live and proclaim the grandeur and beauty of marriage and the joy of being and making a family....

I urge all married couples, therefore, priests and parish communities, as well as movements and associations to let themselves be led by the Word of God, on which rests the foundation of the holy edifice of the family, the domestic Church and the family of God (see _Lumen Gentium_, 6 and 11).

FRANCIS' LETTER
FOR THE EIGHTH WORLD MEETING OF FAMILIES,
PHILADELPHIA,
SEPTEMBER 22–27, 2015

SCRIPTURE

That is why a man leaves his father and mother and clings to his wife, and the two of them become one body.

GENESIS 2:24

Train the young in the way they should go;
even when old, they will not swerve from it.

PROVERBS 22:6

PRAYER

Great and loving God, you provide the ideal relationship within the Holy Trinity. As families we are called to proclaim the love of God in our own marital relationship and to raise our children with a focus on the love of the family. There are many ways to center our family on God, but a regular relationship with your word is a critical means by which we can remain centered on your holy mission for us: proclaiming your name to all and serving as living examples of the perfection of your Trinitarian relational nature. Bless us and grace us, Holy Trinity, with a focus on opening our family's love to the outside world by prioritizing our love for God through your sacred Scripture. Amen.

CHRISTMAS ACTION

Do you incorporate the word of God into your daily life? If not, take a few minutes each evening for the next few weeks before dinner and read a few verses of sacred Scripture for a brief premeal reflection. (The word of God might even inspire some interesting and enlightening conversation during the course of the meal.) Begin viewing your family as a model of God's love. Brainstorm ways in which your family—perhaps through your parish—might proclaim God's love through your words and especially through your actions. See what your parish has to offer for your family as a whole. There might be some all-inclusive activities in which you can participate as a group.

Day

37

Salvation by Faith

On the basis of this sharing in Jesus' way of seeing things, Saint Paul has left us a description of the life of faith. In accepting the gift of faith, believers become a new creation; they receive a new being; as God's children, they are now "sons in the Son." The phrase "Abba, Father," so characteristic of Jesus' own experience, now becomes the core of the Christian experience (see Romans 8:15). The life of faith, as a filial existence, is the acknowledgment of a primordial and radical gift which upholds our lives. We see this clearly in Saint Paul's question to the Corinthians: "What have you that you did not receive?" (1 Corinthians 4:7)....The beginning of salvation is openness to something prior to ourselves, to a primordial gift that affirms life and sustains it in being. Only by being open to and acknowledging this gift can we be transformed, experience salvation and bear good fruit. Salvation by faith means recognizing the primacy of God's gift. As Saint Paul puts it: "By grace you have been saved through faith, and this is not your own doing; it is the gift of God" (Ephesians 2:8).

FRANCIS' ENCYCLICAL LETTER *LUMEN FIDEI*, 19,
JUNE 29, 2013

SCRIPTURE

Since, then, we have the same spirit of faith, according to what is written, "I believed, therefore I spoke," we too believe and therefore speak, knowing that the one who raised the Lord Jesus will raise us also with Jesus and place us with you in his presence.

2 CORINTHIANS 4:13–14

PRAYER

Lord of greatness, of all that is and will be, Lord of deepest intimacy, you of tremendous majesty and deepest knowledge of every person, you have graced us with the great gift of faith. By this gift of faith, with the ability to view you and your creation to the extent that our every experience with you— all that you have created for our joy and pleasure—deepen our intimacy with you. May the deepest relationship we can possibly share with you on this earth lead us to heaven, by your side, and serve as but a foretaste of what awaits us in the exceptional intimacy we will know in the eternity of the afterlife, in your presence, as witness to your beatific vision. Amen.

CHRISTMAS ACTION

Find a quiet place and a few spare minutes for contemplating the state of your faith life at this time. Reflect on as many aspects of your life as you possibly can. How does faith enter into your day-to-day life? In your home economics? Your health and the health of your family? Your relationship with God when everything seems to be going against you? Feelings that God seems absent during such an otherwise highly anticipatory, joyful, and exciting time of the year? Recall that the absence of feeling faith does not mean God is absent. He is, in fact, right beside you always. This is a test of your faith, a test that can strengthen your faith life all the more.

Day
38

Mercy Is the Greatest Virtue

*S*aint Thomas Aquinas taught that the Church's moral teaching has its own "hierarchy" in the virtues and in the acts which proceed from them. What counts above all else is "faith working through love" (Galatians 5:6). Works of love directed to one's neighbour are the most perfect external manifestation of the interior grace of the Spirit: "The foundation of the New Law is in the grace of the Holy Spirit, who is manifested in the faith which works through love." Thomas thus explains that, as far as external works are concerned, mercy is the greatest of all the virtues: "In itself mercy is the greatest of the virtues, since all the others revolve around it and, more than this, it makes up for their deficiencies. This is particular to the superior virtue, and as such it is proper to God to have mercy, through which his omnipotence is manifested to the greatest degree."

FRANCIS' APOSTOLIC EXHORTATION *EVANGELII GAUDIUM*, 37,
NOVEMBER 24, 2013

SCRIPTURE

"Go and learn the meaning of the words, 'I desire mercy, not sacrifice.' I did not come to call the righteous but sinners."

MATTHEW 9:13

If we acknowledge our sins, he is faithful and just and will forgive our sins and cleanse us from every wrongdoing.

1 JOHN 1:9

PRAYER

Heavenly Father, without your ceaseless and unending mercy, we would never have been reunited with you through the vast love that is the hallmark of the mystery of the Incarnation. Adam's sin divided us; your forgiveness, your glorious mercy united us. And even though we sin against you still, we find your mercy awaiting us when we seek it out through the sacrament of reconciliation. Grace us, Lord God, that we might model this mercy you have shown us in our own lives. When I am wronged by someone, please have me immediately recall the fact that you show me mercy at every turn, reminding me that I am called to be merciful to others in light of the constant mercy I have been shown by you. Amen.

CHRISTMAS ACTION

In her diary, St. Faustina Kowalska wrote often of the tremendous, powerful, and unceasing mercy of Jesus Christ. After appearing to her on numerous occasions, he passed along to her a beautiful prayer—the Chaplet of Divine Mercy. This prayer has become more popular in recent years; often, parish groups join together to pray the Chaplet. It is a simple prayer structured upon the beads of the rosary. It is a prayer for mercy; mercy for the person praying, and a petition for mercy on the whole world. Try praying the Chaplet of Divine Mercy. It does not take long and is easy to do. All you need is a rosary; you can look up the prayer method on the internet or purchase a how-to booklet from a religious bookstore.

Day

39

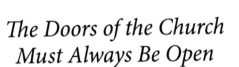

The Doors of the Church Must Always Be Open

The Church is called to be the house of the Father, with doors always wide open. One concrete sign of such openness is that our church doors should always be open, so that if someone, moved by the Spirit, comes there looking for God, he or she will not find a closed door. There are other doors that should not be closed either. Everyone can share in some way in the life of the Church; everyone can be part of the community, nor should the doors of the sacraments be closed for simply any reason. This is especially true of the sacrament which is itself "the door": baptism. The Eucharist, although it is the fullness of sacramental life, is not a prize for the perfect but a powerful medicine and nourishment for the weak..... [T]he Church is...the house of the Father, where there is a place for everyone, with all their problems.

FRANCIS' APOSTOLIC EXHORTATION *EVANGELII GAUDIUM*, 47,
NOVEMBER 24, 2013

SCRIPTURE

Jesus answered and said to them, "Destroy this temple and in three days I will raise it up." The Jews said, "This temple has been under construction for forty-six years, and you will raise it up in three days?" But he was speaking about the temple of his body. Therefore, when he was raised from the dead, his disciples remembered that he had said this, and they came to believe the Scripture and the word Jesus had spoken.

JOHN 2:19–22

PRAYER

Lord, sometimes I am surprised at how selfish I can be. I withdraw from others when they seem to need me; I withdraw from others when I seem to need them. What moves me to act this way? You are always open to me, my dear friend, always there to lift me up, to embrace and comfort me, to grace me with the ability to do great things in your name. And that is what I call on you to do at this time. Grace me, Lord. Create in me an open space for those who seek to find you within me, that they may see your light at my center. Banish my fear, O Lord, and instill within me the faith I seek. This is a faith that is strong, that operates at the center of my being, a faith that holds fast to you, the two of us side by side. Faith is me opening myself to whatever you deem necessary by your will. Move me to open myself in this way. Amen.

CHRISTMAS ACTION

The next time you find yourself in a large group at a parish function or family get-together, pay specific attention to your feelings. Do you feel yourself withdrawing? Do you need to make a special effort to remain open to anyone who may desire to speak with you or confide in you? If this is a challenge, consider removing yourself from the center of the crowd and place yourself on the periphery. In this way you are still open to anyone who may seek God's light and love through you, but you are not putting yourself in a situation where you might feel claustrophobic and pressed upon. (Even Jesus needed to get away from the crowds from time to time!) God calls you to be open to your brother and sister in need, but he also knows you're human.

Day

40

Faith Is to Be Proclaimed

When Saint Paul tells the Christians of Rome that all who believe in Christ make up one body, he urges them not to boast of this; rather, each must think of himself "according to the measure of faith that God has assigned" (Romans 12:3). Those who believe come to see themselves in the light of the faith which they profess: Christ is the mirror in which they find their own image fully realized. And just as Christ gathers to himself all those who believe and makes them his body, so the Christian comes to see himself as a member of this body, in an essential relationship with all other believers. The image of a body does not imply that the believer is simply one part of an anonymous whole, a mere cog in a great machine; rather, it brings out the vital union of Christ with believers and of believers among themselves (see Romans 12:4–5). Christians are "one" (see Galatians 3:28), yet in a way which does not make them lose their individuality; in service to others, they come into their own in the highest degree.

FRANCIS' ENCYCLICAL LETTER *LUMEN FIDEI*, 22,
JUNE 29, 2013

Scripture

For by the grace given to me I tell everyone among you not to think of himself more highly than one ought to think, but to think soberly, each according to the measure of faith that God has apportioned. For as in one body we have many parts, and all the parts do not have the same function, so we, though many, are one body in Christ and individually parts of one another. Since we have gifts that differ according to the grace given to us, let us exercise them: if prophecy, in proportion to the faith; if ministry, in ministering; if one is a teacher, in teaching; if one exhorts, in exhortation; if one contributes, in generosity; if one is over others, with diligence; if one does acts of mercy, with cheerfulness.

ROMANS 12:3–8

Prayer

God of friendship and God of love, you not only desire that our faith deepen our relationship with you, you call each of us to serve as a part, or a member, of the body of Christ. It is in this way that our faith deepens our relationships with every believer who is a member of the body of Christ. This is the reason why you desire that we proclaim our faith: This sacred relationship is not just between you and me. You desire that all believers join together as one as members of one body. Inspire me, dear Jesus, to proclaim my faith in you in words and deeds, and may my actions reflect your love to people I encounter that they may be part of your one body. Amen.

CHRISTMAS ACTION

Today and for all days to follow, let your faith serve you
your shield, your guiding light, a lighthouse for every perso
seeking friendship with God, and the strongest bond you can
possibly form with God in your earthly life, prior to eternity
with him. Know that your faith is more than a feeling that
you feel stronger on some days than on others. Your faith is
a reality that runs deeper than feelings. It is your knowledge
at your core that God is with you and you are a part of the
body of Christ. Know that you have a special place prepared
for you as a member of Christ's body, that you have a place
prepared especially for you in heaven, in the afterlife, forever.